HAL•LEONARD®

VIOLIN
PLAY-ALONG

Lindsey Stirling

AUDIO
ACCESS
INCLUDED

PLAYBACK+
Speed • Pitch • Balance • Loop

CONTENTS

To access audio visit:
www.halleonard.com/mylibrary

Enter Code
7336-1723-7309-9183

ISBN 978-1-4768-7125-7

HAL•LEONARD®
CORPORATION
7777 W. BLUEMOUND RD. P.O. BOX 13819 MILWAUKEE, WI 53213

Visit Hal Leonard Online at
www.halleonard.com

Cover photo: Scott Jarvie

Aaron Ashton, Violin

Audio Arrangements by Peter Deneff and Steve Tanner
Audio Arrangements for "Party Rock Anthem" by
Frank C. Sacramone: Keyboards/Producer, and Jake Bruene: Vocals/Guitar

Michael Jackson Medley

Words and Music by Michael Jackson
Arranged by Lindsey Stirling

WANNA BE STARTIN' SOMETHIN'

SMOOTH CRIMINAL

with intensity

marcato

Party Rock Anthem

Words and Music by Skyler Gordy, Stefan Gordy, David Listenbee and Peter Schroeder
Arranged by Lindsey Stirling, Jake Bruene and Frank Sacramone

Pump It

Words and Music by Will Adams, Allan Pineda, Stacy Ferguson, Thomas Van Musser and Nicholas Roubanis
Arranged by Lindsey Stirling

River Flows in You

By Yiruma
Arranged by Lindsey Stirling

Right Round

Words and Music by Tramar Dillard, Philip Lawrence, Lukasz Gottwald, Allan Grigg, Bruno Mars, Justin Franks, Peter Burns, Stephen Coy, Timothy Lever and Michael Percy
Arranged by Lindsey Stirling

13

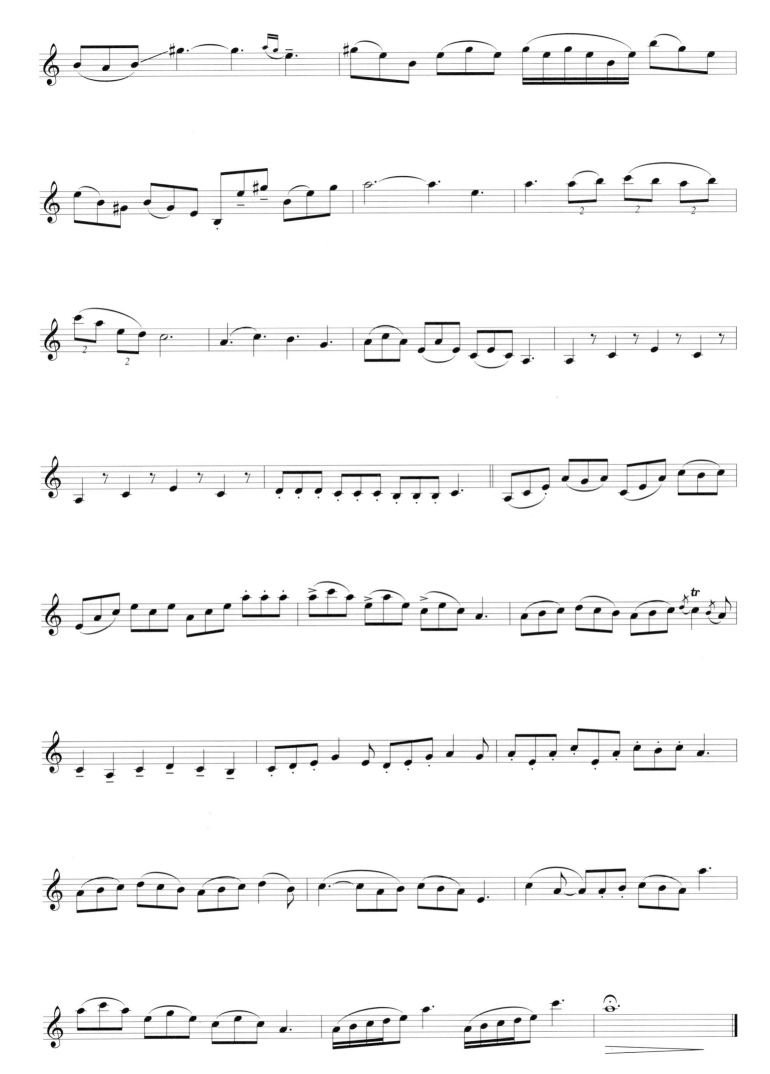

A Thousand Years

from the Summit Entertainment film THE TWILIGHT SAGA: BREAKING DAWN - PART 1

Words and Music by David Hodges and Christina Perri
Arranged by Lindsey Stirling

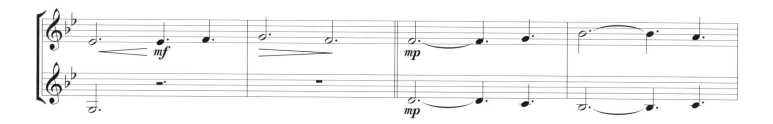

We Found Love

Words and Music by Calvin Harris
Arranged by Lindsey Stirling

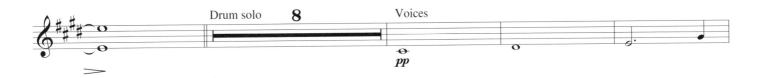

Starships

Words and Music by Nadir Khayat, Onika Maraj, Carl Falk, Wayne Hector and Rami Yacoub
Arranged by Lindsey Stirling

ad lib., with energy!

ad lib., with energy!

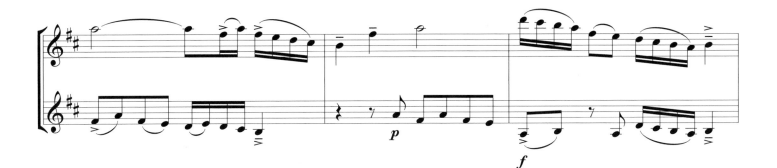